Sleepless Nights

poems by

Maggie Bloomfield

Finishing Line Press
Georgetown, Kentucky

Sleepless Nights

Copyright © 2020 by Maggie Bloomfield
ISBN 978-1-64662-201-6 First Edition
All rights reserved under International and Pan-American Copyright Conventions. No part of this book may be reproduced in any manner whatsoever without written permission from the publisher, except in the case of brief quotations embodied in critical articles and reviews.

ACKNOWLEDGMENTS

I gratefully acknowledge the following publications:

Poetrymagazineonline. My Father's Hat, B. John, 1979
Grabbing the Apple. Sex
Oberon. "Fog"
Bards Annual, 2016. Another Season
Nassau County Poet Laureate Review, 2017. Thoughts during Insomnia in Florence
Suffolk County Poetry Review, 2016. Woman in the Moment
Suffolk County Poetry Review, 2018 On Re-reading John Donne's "The Flea"
Performance Poets Association, Volume 20. Ice Harvest
Performance Poets Association, Volume 21, For My Journey to the End of the World

Publisher: Leah Maines
Editor: Christen Kincaid
Cover Art: Carol Tauser
Author Photo: Thomas Kochie

Printed in the USA on acid-free paper.
Order online: www.finishinglinepress.com
also available on amazon.com

Author inquiries and mail orders:
Finishing Line Press
P. O. Box 1626
Georgetown, Kentucky 40324
U. S. A.

Table of Contents

Thoughts during Insomnia in Florence 1

Mountains 2

Sex 3

My Mother's Drawer 4

Missing Children 5

Collections 6

On Waking 8

Dissolution 9

My Father's Hat 10

Woman in the Moment 11

High School Reunion (that My Ex-Boyfriend Didn't Attend) 12

Ice Harvest 14

Update 15

B. John, 1979 16

For My Journey to the End of the World 17

Childhood Should Be More 18

My Mother's Music Box after the Fire 19

"Fog" 20

Diminutive 22

On Re-reading John Donne's "The Flea" 24

The Lability of Lobsters 25

After the Biopsy 26

Another Season 27

Sleepless Nights 28

Lying on the Beach on a Starry Night 29

*Dedicated to
Michael Gari,
my husband and my rock*

Thoughts during Insomnia in Florence

I hopscotched last
on these cobblestones
in spikes and mini-dresses,
long golden tresses,
trailed by a succession
of Davids,
who pinched and petted,
followed me into bars,
embraced me under stars
on the Ponte Vecchio,
begging me to never go,
then broke my heart,
or was that Art?

Now, in Uggs and Nikes,
and far too many clothes,
I read poetry,
reflect
on how history flows,
an unfinished fresco,
the signature my own,
while David gazes past me,
eyes blank as stone.

Mountains

move me,
even mere stratigraphic ridges,
flat-chested imitations of Mt. Kilimanjaro's
perfectly formed peaks and valleys
plunging and rising.

Riding my mother's lap in early childhood,
or sitting across from her
at the kitchen table,
I stared at the graceful crevice just above the buttons
of her ubiquitous housedress,
where hill met valley.
I longed to know what lay beneath,
what mysteries lurked in that darkness,
tunneling away from sunlight.

I often gazed out my bedroom window
at the Alleghenies looking back at me,
modest, but solid.
Whatever secrets lay in the shadows,
I would always feel safe.

Sex

Crabs mate face to face,
claws entwined,
eyes filled with the appearance
of strong feeling.
First, he dances
on pointy little claws
to lure the mature
female
onto her back,
both having shed their skins
at this point.
Exposed, vulnerable,
they clutch and buck and moan
like lovers everywhere,
the male peering
brainlessly into madam's eyes
with some crustacean impulse
of "I love her"
or
"God, I want to pin her,"
While, beneath him,
she muses primordially,
"He's a terrible dancer,
but I want to have his children."

My Mother's Drawer

I entered your room
though I was forbidden,
opened the magical drawer,
to solve the mystery

though I was forbidden.
My eyes widened at the sight.
I longed to solve the mystery,
be privy to the secret.

My eyes widened at the sight,
lipsticks, rouges, polishes, pencils of kohl.
Privy to the secret.
I swooned to mingling aromas,

lipsticks, rouges, polishes, pencils of kohl,
all powdered with rosy dust.
I swooned to mingling aromas,
fragrance of you

powdered with rosy dust.
I clumsily put on rouge, lipstick,
fragrance of you.
This is the me I will become.

I clumsily put on rouge, lipstick,
tissued telltale fingers.
This is the me I will become.
The me of you

tissued telltale fingers,
opened the magical drawer.
The me of you
entered your room.

Missing Children

In the months
when you wouldn't talk to me,
I learned that blood owns no one,
merely passes on.

Collections

My collection of small pitchers
does nothing to postpone my death,
though the trio of ivory teases.
The smallest contains the soft accoutrement
to a lonely cup of coffee,
the medium embraces the creamy smoothness
of hours spent
with a friend or lover
over tea for two,
the largest explodes with tabletop festivity,
splashes on banquettes, clothes,
hastily noted phone numbers.

My miniature Willow commemorates
a certain Seventh Avenue barista
while a memory of Azuma
and a lost friendship brim from the azure flowered.

The gilt-edged hotel beige is
product of Fish's Eddy's,
Pottery Barn,
sober anniversary loot, or stolen
from a restaurant
during an elongated term of service.

Autumn-striped and signed ceramic,
perfect fit for the carry-on
back from Florence,
streamlined,
unlike the painted rosy confection
pressed into the waving, tremulous hand
of my great grandmother
by her waving, tremulous friend,
as she boarded from England
to the New World.

Sentinels, they perch
on shelves, countertops, tables,
trapped with matching sugar bowls
in backlit china closets,
maps of my universe, marks
of significance and insignificance,
informing the narrative.

My collection of small pitchers does nothing to postpone my death.

On Waking

This New York City apartment
faces the strangely altered
downtown skyline.
A yellow monster crane
stands visible atop
an unfinished Everest,
fodder for errant lunatics,
rogue pilots,
the odd postalpath.
Genius erector set,
miles high
(in the morning sky).
I picture hardhats in a huddle,
organizing a Tyrannosaurus.

Building up there,
it must be hard to breathe.
Who connects the two hundred foot arm
reaching for that helicopter?
Has anything ever looked so precarious,
other than my life,
this morning?

Dissolution

I.

Sadness flows from your body like blood.
I blink and our connection breaks.
Good times vanish from our table like food.
Sadness flows from your body like blood,
our bountiful harvest rotting in mud,
once bursting forth in brilliant display.
Sadness flows from your body like blood.
I blink and our connection breaks.

II

The empty bed turns me dead with pale.
What drove our souls to such divide?
Devastation remains for those who fail.
the empty bed turns me dead with pale.
Destruction finishes this fairy tale,
dismal demise of plans of promise.
The empty bed turns me dead with pale.
What drove our souls to such divide?

III

First trauma is loss of touch and talk.
Each transformation widens the abyss,
illusions shattered, scattered on the walk.
First trauma is loss of touch and talk.
Tremulous tenderness, now sullen sulk,
what we each loved now tedious.
First trauma is loss of touch and talk.
Each transformation widens the abyss.

My Father's Hat

Something in a poem about touching his father's hat,
and I was transported
back to a home, a house I left
when I was ten,
trying to recall
where we hung our coats,
remembering the feel of my father's hats,
unsure if he ever wore one.
I know he ate yogurt,
and drank buttermilk on occasion
and no one else has ever
made me laugh
as much
as he.

Woman in the Moment

I watch as I wait for my latte.
The lipstick slides
across her mouth,
a Barbie Doll tennis match
I follow,

back …and forth,
back… and forth,

mesmerized
by her concentration;
the balanced compact,
impeccable outlining,
the practiced swivel
of burnished tube,
the protrusion of plum wax.

The shine blinds.

I am entranced.

With focus like hers,
we could effect world peace.

High School Reunion (that My Ex-Boyfriend Didn't Attend)

Morning closes, wet and hot.
My t-shirt clings, mosquitoes thrive.
I am stuck to reflection's sticky spot.

> *The long, long lashes*
> *that turned chemistry class*
> *into chemistry class.*
>
> *Parked in your aqua Ford Skyliner*
> *Burgers at the drive-thru*
> *Hungers at the drive-in.*
>
> *The black orchid for prom*
> *pinned on my pink tulle princess dress*
> *Mother incredulous, "A black orchid?"*

Adolescence danced to
"There you are, Little Star,"
Smart, hot, young, we
vowed lifetime connection.
Ambition lured you to
the temperate west.
I lingered, loving seasons best.

> *Lithe fingers, genius inventions*
> *earn the toys and wealth you crave.*
> *Music, words, enactments,*
> *boys and booze diffuse*
> *my modest gifts, an unfinished*
> *collage of artistry.*

These morning groves,
foggy and blazing,
contain me.
My pen resolutely scurries
beneath clouds
that shift, clear,
thrust and parry
with "What-ifs,"
with the foolish longing
to have you here.

Ice Harvest

Chilled bones ache with each reduced degree.
Already summer seems far-off.
I miss the sunny ocean's balm,
yet snow on sand calms,
bringing winter's dreams of cozy fires,
quilts that warm and soothe us.

Our thermostat demands control by me.
You're always lowering it one more degree.
This dance of heat
chills our shared domesticity
until we laugh.

Dear God, the levity is wondrous,
softening the brittle, winter me,
warming you as well,
flushing my pallid cheeks,
fleshing out the fragile skeleton
that holds us.

Winter's bluster crackles
into edgy conversation.
The easy autumn banter
freezes into sullen murmurs.

Love that blooms in spring and summer
drifts to fields of frost.
Seasons flow melodically
in moody rhythms,
temperate and intemperate,
Brahms darkness, Mozart's light.

What binds us to each other is a mystery,
an unremembered history of passion and pretense,
ephemeral as a breeze,
soft as the snow that will cover you and me.

Update

I'm sorry.
Raspberry jam
on white paper
eaten for lunch
shat for breakfast
Song dissonant
as heavy metal
or the Senate
bilboinking
on healthcare
while Rome
next to Liberty
goes up in flames

>   *Where is the cinema with the unhappy ending?*
>   *Where have all the eggcreams gone?*

Eisenberg ticky-tacky sandwiches
over the fucking rainbow coalition
city thrown up by ocean
where dunes are trampled
for the sheer pleasure
of pleasure sheared.

B. John 1979

B. John does his funny duckwalk across Sheridan Square.
He lost his toes in the park one icy night
when his soggy head told him his bench was always warm.
At St. Vincent's they took the blue stuff that was left.
    They already had his teeth
    and most of his brain,
put it all in the envelope marked "No hope."
But B. John fooled 'em,
He duckwalked back downtown, and there he goes,
murmuring fuzzy prayers and dreaming of comfortable shoes.

For My Journey to the End of the World

I will carry my pencil
I will carry my blue hat
I will carry my Mason Pearson hairbrush
I will carry my antique violin
I will carry my soy candle
I will carry a carafe of pomegranate juice
    and a china cup
    and a lemon
I will carry birdseed
I will carry my silk flowered scarf
I will carry a brown paper sac
    and twine
        to tie up the brown paper sac
I will carry dried apricots
    in my brown paper sac
I will carry a lace collar, a linen handkerchief
    a poem by Emily Dickinson
    and a dozen macarons
I will carry an Elvis Presley stamp
I will carry a gauze bandage
I will carry the piece of my heart
    you left me

Childhood Should Be More

This child should be
recalled,
the notes she penned,
her plans each day,
dotting each "i"
of her journal,
the corner of the
dinner table
her counterfeit desk.
She reads and writes,
the fountain pen
never empty,
kept as sharp as
Aunt Flo's tongue
lashing at this
persistence in
discovering words,
a voice
to be heard,
acknowledged,
unerased.
In her seventh year,
an orphan,
her future forged
by elders' hands,
she clears the dishes,
leaving a
dark oak surface
her sole refuge.

My Mother's Music Box after the Fire

Talcum
never tainted
your milkweed puff,
nor did the ash
that trashed
your rosy
Victoriana skin,
the thousand faces made,
all looking
like someone
I wanted to be.

Who chose
the unidentified tune
inside
as you?

"Fog"

                        Vagueness.
like waking, or not quite
        waking
                from dreamless sleep   memory
                                disappears

                emerges

                      cal
              rrati   ly
  e

damaged slides on an old viewfinder

            namescondense   e v a porat e

    faces lack depth
                                expression

    robotic visits from another universe eyes, noses generic
                unidentifiable
                dampness
                exudes
                from
  pores tissues   wads of cotton
            chaffing
              thighs

        speech fails with the
           slipping away
                  of words

songs from youth surface   clear
              as churchbells   perfect melodies, harmonica
                     mastered a lifetime ago

                recognition glances by
    the peal of your laughter
                              a longing to return
                                        anywhere.

I want to make love to you one more time.

Diminutive

Crayfish, crawfish
no fish

Cambarellus Diminutus
tiny lobster,

pincers poised
delicately

for prey.
Swimmerets jete

through ponds
of clarity

or amble criss-cross
over stones,

pry sustenance
from rock crevices.

Antennae eyes
gracefully stalk,

flipping fabulously
backwards,

calisthenics
away

from ducks, turtles,
our appetites,

pinch the hand
that would devour

the molting softness,
vulnerable

exoskeleton
notwithstanding

the fall to autumn sex,
spring harvest,

the "in berry" mother's
ripe cluster

of translucent,
dark eggs,

minute
sonograms.

While parents sleep,
babies burst forth,

cavort in sunlight
eager, new,

oppositional,

like progeny
everywhere.

On Re-reading John Donne's "The Flea"

The flea as metaphor
served John Donne well,
a fact our history proves sure.
His flea,
a symbol of seductive passion,
was pretty hot,
subverting much of Jacobean fashion.

These days, most fleas
are relegated to annoyance, a
ditty by Shel Silverstein
or part of Ogden's Nashery,
while Donne made itchiness erotic,
high art without a hint of trashery.

If some romantic dude read
Donne's erotic words to me,
I'd probably ménage a trois
with Dude and Mr. Flea.

The Lability of Lobsters

Lobsters possess serotonin.
Unlike the neurological
spurts of joy
that light up our human brains
after a solid workout,
the eensy lobster neurotransmitters
propel aggression.

Lobsters fight,
mano a mano,
claw to claw,
spindly limbs tensed
for balance, carapaces colliding.
They box and batter,
and as in all battles, someone
wins and someone loses.

The winner struts through lobster land,
triumphant as Ali after Liston.
Antennae sparkle with electrical
volts of joyful neurotransmittance.

        while loser lobster, serotonin quashed
forever, retreats
in shame.
No proper parenting or validation will
bring him back to the ring.
He will bottom-feed for the duration.

Serotonin makes lobster meat tough.
We love to eat the losers.

After the Biopsy

In the projection of my death,
while I waited to learn I'm not dying,
there were tons of flowers,
hundreds of mourners,
my ashes in a small,
but beautifully appointed container.
Tears flowed,
laughter was remembered,
accomplishments were reiterated admiringly,
and I was there, of course,
enjoying it all.

Another Season

Another season fades, leaving
serpentine vines, spiced residues.

Uneaten fruits crumble damply
in shadows, unmattering back

from an island
of summer.

A now
molders underfoot.

In black subterranean caves,
roots and sealed seeds
flow toward fall.

Time's measure flares
boisterous, chafes,

like us,
longing to stay.

Sleepless Nights

Pigs sing on top of pillows, piling up plums in my mouth as I plow through Purgatory. Pythagoras counts rainbows. Dawn blinks, I sink, but stand up, go on, no naps, no food, no calls, distraught on all fronts. I want, I want, I pray, my day fills with muddy thoughts, insanity, loss, torn clothing I toss in a dirty pool. Try, try, go away. Stay. I am ill. I could kill. Worlds of mad, sad. No glad today. Only worry, hurry, daylight running away. Will you stay through night, kiss this angst away?

Stay.

Lying on the Beach on a Starry Night

An errant star trails sparks through velvet skies,
swathing a lustrous path through ocean's night.
Cool sand, soft cushion for my weary eyes
to rest and follow its ephemeral flight.

I long to fly that stratospheric course,
to gaze upon myself light years below,
beside torrential, pewter force—my speck,
devoid of clear trajectory or glow.

Oh comets, planets, meteors, connect.
Collide in fire and fury as you fly.
Throw sparks of immortality, protect
no more God's secret: how to never die.

The ebb and flow that carries all to sea
will capture shooting stars, the world, and me.

Maggie Bloomfield is a poet, lyricist, performer, and psychotherapist. She is author of *Trains of Thought*, (Local Gems Press, 2016), and has won first place three times in the Performance Poets Association (PPA) annual contest on Long Island. Her poems and essays have been published, in *The Southampton Press (TSR), Oberon, Psychoanalytic Perspectives, Grabbing the Apple, The East Hampton Star, PoetryMagazine.com, Psychoanalytical Perspectives, The Montauk Anthology, The Suffolk County Poetry Review, The Nassau Review, Local Gems,* and *Bards Initiative*.

Maggie's lyrics won an EMMY for contributions to Sesame Street. Maggie began writing poetry in 2007 and received an MFA from Stony Brook, Southampton in 2013. Maggie runs writing workshops, presents, and performs spoken word, alone, and with other "Poets of Well-Being," in rehabs, at national writing conferences, and creative therapy conferences. She has performed spoken word at The Café Nuyorican in NYC and at The Green Mill in Chicago, and co-hosts Poetry Street, a monthly poetry venue, in Riverhead, NY.

Sober for more than four decades, Maggie, with poet Susan Dingle, wrote and performed a one-act play, *BREAK OUT!* based on their parallel misadventures on Broadway and in Hollywood during the 70's. It was produced at the Southampton Cultural Center in 2016, and was part of the LI Fringe Festival in Riverhead, NY in 2017.

www.maggiebloomfield.com

www.ingramcontent.com/pod-product-compliance
Lightning Source LLC
LaVergne TN
LVHW041508070426
835507LV00012B/1417